LET'S FIND OUT! PRIMARY SOURCES

THE U.S. CONSTITUTION

KATHERINE MANGER

Britannica
Educational Publishing

IN ASSOCIATION WITH

ROSEN
EDUCATIONAL SERVICES

Published in 2017 by Britannica Educational Publishing (a trademark of Encyclopædia Britannica, Inc.) in association with The Rosen Publishing Group, Inc.
29 East 21st Street, New York, NY 10010

Distributed exclusively by Rosen Publishing.
To see additional Britannica Educational Publishing titles, go to rosenpublishing.com.

First Edition

Britannica Educational Publishing
J.E. Luebering: Executive Director, Core Editorial
Mary Rose McCudden: Editor, Britannica Student Encyclopedia

Rosen Publishing
Nicholas Croce: Editor
Nelson Sá: Art Director
Nicole Russo: Designer
Cindy Reiman: Photography Manager
Karen Huang: Photo Researcher

Library of Congress Cataloging-in-Publication Data

Names: Manger, Katherine, author.
Title: The U.S. Constitution / Katherine Manger.
Description: First edition. | New York : Britannica Educational Publishing, in association with The Rosen Publishing Group, 2017. | Series: Let's find out! Primary sources | Includes bibliographical references and index. | Audience: Grades 1-4.
Identifiers: LCCN 2016028179 | ISBN 9781508103974 (library bound) | ISBN 9781508103981 (paperback) | ISBN 9781508103202 (6-pack)
Subjects: LCSH: United States. Constitution—Juvenile literature | Constitutional history—United States—Juvenile literature. | United States—Politics and government—1783-1789—Juvenile literature.
Classification: LCC KF4550 .M263 2017 | DDC 342.7302—dc23
LC record available at https://lccn.loc.gov/2016028179

Manufactured in China

CONTENTS

Looking at Primary Sources

Primary sources are artifacts, documents, or other sources of information that were created at the time under study. Some examples of primary sources are documents (such as newspapers, letters, and journals), photographs, objects, and even buildings. The study of primary sources gives us a clear view into history.

The United States Constitution is on display in the National Archives in Washington, D.C.

These are the front doors to the Supreme Court building in Washington, D.C.

VOCABULARY

A **constitution** is a set of basic laws by which a country or state is governed.

The United States **Constitution** is a primary source. The main text of the Constitution is made up of an introduction (called the preamble) and seven articles. Twenty-seven amendments, or changes, have been added to the Constitution since it was created in 1789. The first ten amendments are called the Bill of Rights.

The Constitution describes the branches of the government and their separate powers. The powers work together to form a strong united nation that promotes growth and prosperity.

A First of Its Kind

The United States is younger than many other countries. However, it has the oldest written constitution among the major nations of the world.

The United States Constitution was the first in history to specifically limit the powers that the government would be able to have over its citizens. It is the most basic set of laws of the United States.

The Constitution was a replacement for an even older set of rules called the Articles of

This is the title page of the Articles of Confederation.

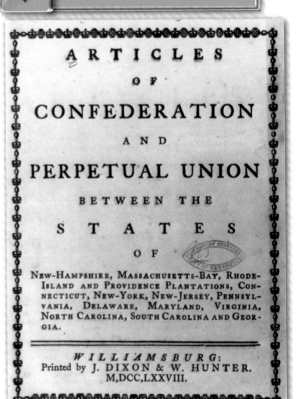

ARTICLES

OF

CONFEDERATION

AND

PERPETUAL UNION

BETWEEN THE

STATES

OF

NEW-HAMPSHIRE, MASSACHUSETTS-BAY, RHODE-ISLAND AND PROVIDENCE PLANTATIONS, CONNECTICUT, NEW-YORK, NEW-JERSEY, PENNSYLVANIA, DELAWARE, MARYLAND, VIRGINIA, NORTH CAROLINA, SOUTH CAROLINA AND GEORGIA.

WILLIAMSBURG:

Printed by J. DIXON & W. HUNTER.

M,DCC,LXXVIII.

Confederation. The Articles were written in 1776–77, when the United States first became a country. But there were problems. By 1785, many citizens saw the Articles of Confederation as a failure.

THINK ABOUT IT

The Constitution is the founding document of the laws of the United States. Why is the Constitution necessary?

George Washington, Alexander Hamilton, John Jay, James Madison, and other leaders repeatedly said that the government should be strengthened. In 1787 representatives from twelve of the thirteen states met in Philadelphia, Pennsylvania. They wrote a completely new document—the Constitution.

This painting shows several of the writers of the U.S. Constitution.

THE CONSTITUTIONAL CONVENTION · 1787

7

The Origins of the Constitution

The writers of the Constitution were inspired by other founding documents in history. The Magna Carta and the English Bill of Rights were a great influence. The Magna Carta was signed in 1215. It gave certain rights to some people in England and required the king to follow the law. The English Bill of Rights of 1689 limited the power of the **monarch** and granted more power to Parliament.

Vocabulary

A **monarch** is a person (such as a king or queen) who rules a kingdom or empire.

This is a manuscript of the Magna Carta, dating from 1215.

Documents from the American colonies also influenced the writers of the Constitution. The Mayflower Compact was an agreement made in 1620. It was signed by the people who founded the Plymouth colony. The compact was the first plan for self-government in the American colonies.

Between 1775 and 1787 every state except Rhode Island and Connecticut had written at least one state constitution. These experiments by the states offered many helpful lessons to the delegates who met for the Constitutional Convention in Philadelphia in 1787.

A painting shows the Mayflower Compact being signed in 1620 on the *Mayflower*.

The Constitutional Convention

A number of small steps led to the convention at which the Constitution was written. The first was a meeting in 1785 between representatives of Virginia and Maryland, called the Alexandria Conference. This conference was held to settle disputes over the navigation of the Potomac River. George Washington and James Madison took the lead in calling this meeting.

Next Madison called together all the states to write an amendment to the Articles of Confederation. This convention was in Annapolis, Maryland, in 1786. However, only five states sent representatives,

Independence Hall is where the Constitution was signed.

This painting is called *Signing of the Constitution*.

and they all had different opinions. Madison and Alexander Hamilton **persuaded** the representatives to issue a call for a general convention of all the states. It would be held in Philadelphia, Pennsylvania, on the second Monday of May 1787. This was to be the Constitutional Convention.

In the summer of 1787, the Constitutional Convention began. Fifty-five men from twelve states met to revise the Articles of Confederation. The Convention was a secret session of argument, debate, and compromise that produced the Constitution of the United States.

THE GREAT COMPROMISE

The delegates who attended the Constitutional Convention had different opinions on many issues. One important issue was how many representatives each state should have in the new legislature. The legislature is the part of the government that makes laws. The large states agreed on the Virginia Plan, which assigned representatives based on each state's population. The smaller states preferred the New Jersey Plan, which gave each state the same number of representatives.

The present-day U.S. Senate meets in Washington, D.C.

Roger Sherman, a delegate from Connecticut, proposed a plan to have a two-house legislature. The legislature would be made up of a Senate and a House of Representatives.

The Senate would have the same number of representatives—two—from each state. That would satisfy states with smaller populations. In the House of Representatives the number of members for each state would be **proportional** to the state's population. That means that states with many people would have more representatives than states with fewer people. That satisfied the states with larger populations. This solution came to be known as the Great Compromise.

VOCABULARY

Proportional means matching in size or amount.

The U.S. House has 435 members today. Fifty-three are from California, the most populous state.

"WE THE PEOPLE"

The preamble of the Constitution introduces the basic principles of the document. It says, "We the People of the United States, in Order to form a more perfect Union, establish Justice, insure domestic Tranquility, provide for the common defense, promote the general welfare, and secure the Blessings of Liberty to ourselves and our **Posterity**, do ordain and establish this Constitution for the United States of America."

VOCABULARY

Posterity is all future generations, or people in the future.

The original copy of the U.S. Constitution is in Washington, D.C.

The Thomas Jefferson Memorial is located in Washington, D.C.

This passage means that the people of the United States desired to bring all the states together to make a better nation. It says that the Constitution was written to establish justice and peace for all its citizens and to take care of the citizens. It also says that the Constitution should protect the freedoms of the present and future generations.

THE SEPARATION OF POWER

The writers of the Constitution wanted government leaders to share power with each other. So they separated the government into three equal branches. The first three articles of the Constitution define the roles of the three branches of government.

Article I, Section 1, of the Constitution states: "All legislative Powers herein granted shall be vested in a Congress of the United States, which shall consist of a Senate and House of Representatives." The legislative branch, or Congress, makes laws.

Congress meets in the building called the United States Capitol.

COMPARE AND CONTRAST

All three branches of government are responsible for laws in some way. Compare and contrast the different ways.

Article II begins "The executive Power shall be vested in a President of the United States of America." The president executes the laws of the nation, or makes sure the laws are followed.

Article III begins "The judicial Power of the United States, shall be vested in one supreme Court." The Supreme Court is the highest court in the nation. It is in charge of figuring out what the laws mean.

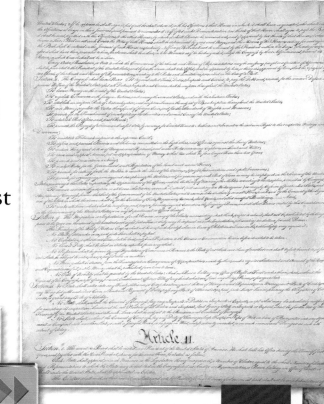

Article II appears on the second page of the U.S. Constitution.

The main responsibility of the legislative branch is to make and approve laws. In addition, the legislative branch sets and collects taxes. It is also in charge of opening post offices and roads, maintaining the military, and declaring war.

The president is the leader of the executive branch. It is his or her job to enforce the laws and to choose judges, ambassadors, and

The president of the United States lives and works in the White House.

military officers. The president is commander of the nation's military. The president also meets with ambassadors from other nations and signs agreements with other countries.

The judicial branch is a system of courts. The Supreme Court is the highest court in the country. The Supreme Court has the power to undo the decisions of lower courts. It also has the power to overturn laws that do not agree with the U.S. Constitution.

The Supreme Court building is on Capitol Hill in Washington, D.C.

A System of Checks and Balances

The three branches of government divide the government's duties so that each branch has some power over the others. This is called a system of checks and balances.

Each branch of government is able to prevent actions by the other branches. In this way, no one branch can grow too powerful.

For example, the president can veto, or reject, laws passed by Congress. Congress can override the

John Adams helped form the system of checks and balances we have today.

IN GOD WE TRUST

President Obama delivers a speech to Congress.

president's veto if at least two-thirds of the members of each house vote to do so.

The people who wrote the Constitution added the checks and balances because they wanted to prevent tyranny. Tyranny is unfair treatment by people with power over others.

THINK ABOUT IT

How does the president's power to veto and Congress's power to override the veto prevent tyranny?

The Supreme Court

The Supreme Court is the highest court of the United States. It is the only court established by the Constitution. The Supreme Court has two main responsibilities: to rule on legal cases and to decide what the Constitution means.

The language of the Constitution has not changed since it was written. Amendments have been added to address certain issues, but the text of the Constitution

Pictured here is the interior of the courtroom of the Supreme Court.

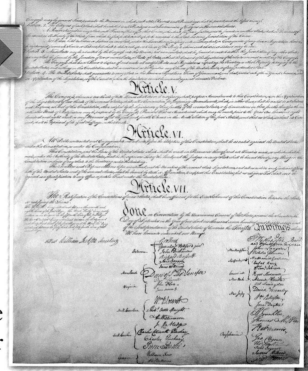

Articles V, VI, and VII appear on the last page of the U.S. Constitution.

has not changed. People do not always agree about what those words mean, though. Therefore, it is the responsibility of the Supreme Court to interpret the law for the public.

The Supreme Court provides that the Constitution and the laws made to support the Constitution "shall be the supreme Law of the Land."

THINK ABOUT IT

Five of the delegates at the Constitutional Convention went on to become Supreme Court justices. Why do you think they were chosen?

The Bill of Rights

The Constitution is sometimes called a "living document." This means that it was designed to change, or be amended, as the beliefs of society change over time. However, changing the Constitution is not easy to do. Two-thirds of each house of Congress and three-fourths of the states must approve every amendment.

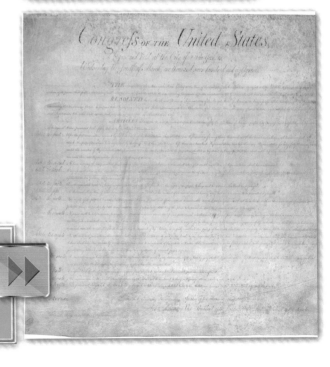

The original Bill of Rights had twelve amendments, but only ten were approved.

James Madison wrote the first ten amendments of the Constitution, known as the Bill of Rights. Basic principles of human liberty are spelled out in those ten amendments. The Bill of Rights protects the rights of the individual by limiting the government's power. It reflects the principles of "life, liberty, and the pursuit of happiness" stated in the Declaration of Independence.

Only seventeen other amendments have been added to the Constitution since the Bill of Rights was approved in 1791.

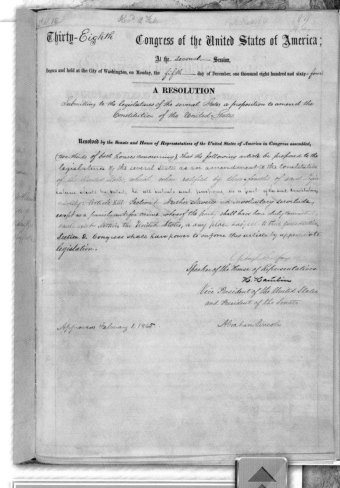

The 13th Amendment to the Constitution made slavery illegal.

RATIFICATION OF THE CONSTITUTION

By September 1787 the work of the Constitutional Convention was nearly done. After months of debate between the delegates, the essential points of the Constitution were written down, reviewed, and edited. On September 17, 1787, it was signed by thirty-nine members. It was ready for the people to approve or reject. One section of the Constitution says that nine of the thirteen states had to **ratify** the document before it could be established.

For Mr Church from her sister Elizabeth Hamilton

THE

FEDERALIST;

A COLLECTION

OF

E S S A Y S,

WRITTEN IN FAVOUR OF THE

NEW CONSTITUTION,

AS AGREED UPON BY THE FEDERAL CONVENTION,
SEPTEMBER 17, 1787.

IN TWO VOLUMES.

VOL. I.

NEW-YORK:

PRINTED AND SOLD BY J. AND A. M'LEAN,
No. 41, HANOVER-SQUARE.

VOCABULARY

To **ratify** means to make a document official by signing it or voting for it.

 The Federalist papers (1787–8) argued for the Constitution.

People celebrate the 200th anniversary of the signing of the Constitution.

One by one the states held conventions to debate the Constitution. People were divided over one main issue. That issue was how much power the new government should have.

The Constitution gave the United States a federal system. In a federal system, different levels of government share power. In the United States, the national, or federal, government shares power with the governments of the states. Even under this system of sharing power, the national government gained more power under the new Constitution than it had had under the Articles of Confederation.

Alexander Hamilton helped write the Federalist papers.

People who supported the federal system were called Federalists. Other people feared that the new national government would be too strong. They were called Anti-Federalists. They thought the Constitution should guarantee the rights of individuals.

Three of the writers of the Constitution wrote a series of essays to promote the new constitution. The essays became known as the Federalist papers. They explained the Constitution for the people and helped convince the states to vote for the document. By June 1788 nine of the states had ratified the Constitution, and it became official.

A young boy views the original copy of the Constitution.

Several of the states that ratified the Constitution thought that amendments should be added to address the rights of individuals. The amendments, which became known as the Bill of Rights, were added in 1791.

THINK ABOUT IT

The Federalist papers were printed in newspapers anonymously, meaning that the authors did not want to reveal their names. Why do you think that they wanted to remain anonymous?

GLOSSARY

artifact An object created by people that teaches something about the past or a particular culture.

compromise An agreement reached after a dispute in which both sides give up some demands.

delegate A person sent with power to act for another.

executive Related to the carrying out of laws and the conduct of public and national affairs.

federal Related to a form of government in which power is shared between a central government and individual states, provinces, or territories.

judicial Related to courts of law or judges.

legislative Having the power to make laws.

liberty The condition of those who are able to act and speak freely.

override To make something no longer valid.

population The number of people living in a place.

principle A moral rule or belief that helps you know what is right and wrong and that influences your actions.

prosperity The state of being successful.

pursuit The act of trying to get or do something.

session A whole series of meetings.

society People living together in organized communities with shared laws, traditions, and values.

tranquility The state of being calm.

treaties An official agreement that is made between two or more countries or groups.

veto To officially reject a proposed law, or the power of an official to decide that a new law will not be approved.

FOR MORE INFORMATION

Books

Cheney, Lynne V., and Greg Harlin. *We the People: The Story of Our Constitution.* New York, NY: Simon & Schuster Books for Young Readers, 2012.

Otfinoski, Steven. *The U.S. Constitution, Bill of Rights, and a New Nation.* North Mankato, MN: Capstone Press, 2013.

Richmond, Benjamin. *What Are the Three Branches of the Government?: And Other Questions About the U.S. Constitution.* New York, NY: Sterling Children's Books, 2014.

Sobel, Syl, and Denise Gilgannon. *The U.S. Constitution and You.* Hauppauge, NY: Barron's Educational Series, 2012.

Swain, Gwenyth. *Documents of Freedom: a Look at the Declaration of Independence, the Bill of Rights, and the U.S. Constitution.* Minneapolis, MN: Lerner Publications, 2012.

Turner, Juliette. *Our Constitution Rocks.* Grand Rapids, MI: Zondervan, 2012.

Websites

Because of the changing nature of internet links, Rosen Publishing has developed an online list of websites related to the subject of this book. This site is updated regularly. Please use this link to access the list:

http://www.rosenlinks.com/LFO/usc

INDEX